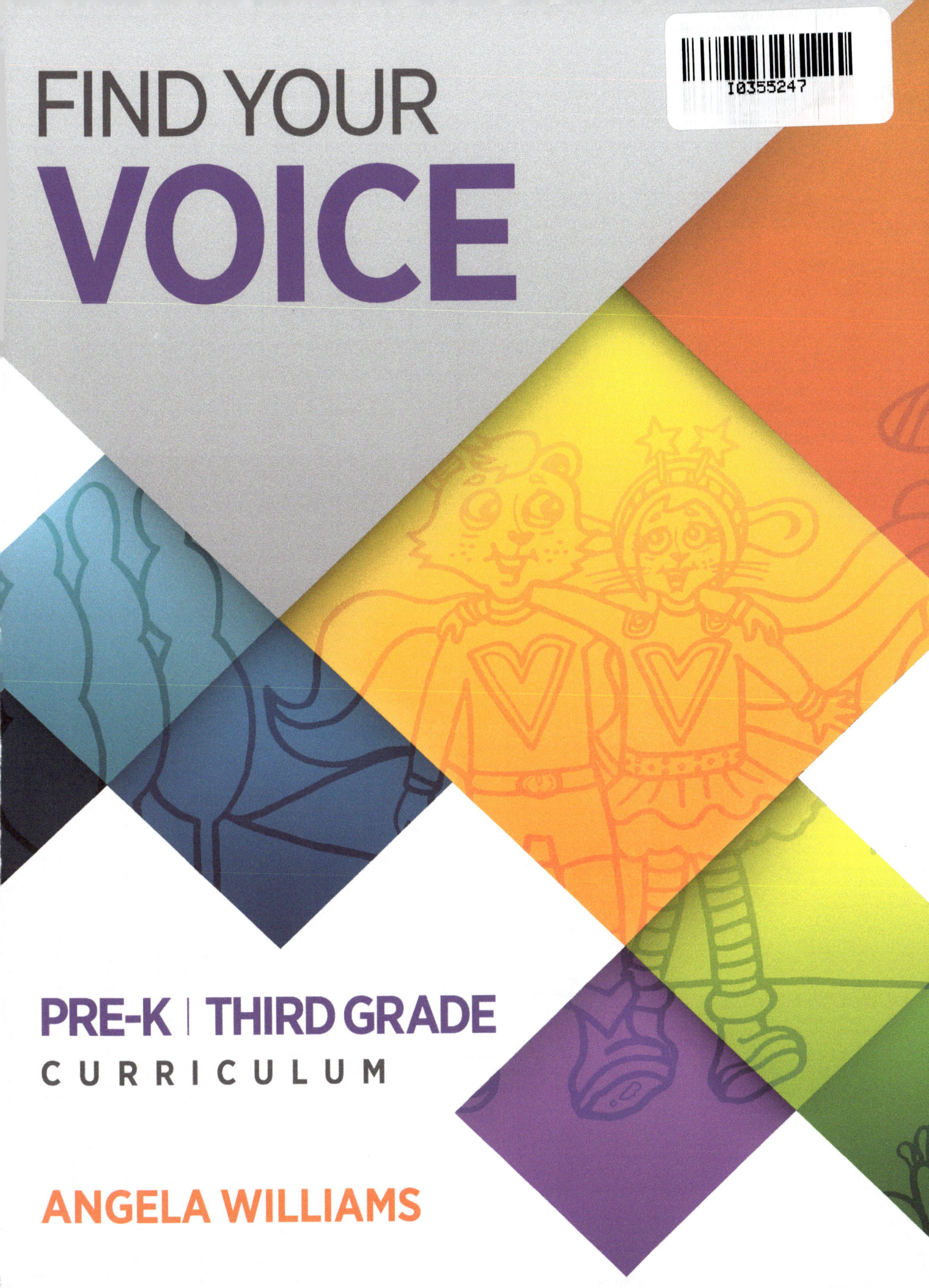

Thank you to Iris Davis, Ashley Chupp, Kristin N. Tanner, and Lorin Cook for their contribution to *Find Your Voice Curriculum*.

BOOKLOGIX
Alpharetta, Georgia

The resources contained within this book are provided for informational purposes only and should not be used to replace the specialized training and professional judgment of a healthcare or mental healthcare professional. Angela's Voice and the publisher of this work cannot be held responsible for the use of the information provided. Always consult a licensed mental health professional before making any decision regarding treatment of yourself or others.

Copyright © 2023 by Angela's Voice

All rights reserved. No part of this book may be reproduced or transmitted in any form or by any means, electronic or mechanical, including photocopying, recording, or any information storage and retrieval system, without permission in writing from the author.

ISBN: 978-1-61005-998-5

This ISBN is the property of BookLogix for the express purpose of sales and distribution of this title. The content of this book is the property of the copyright holder only. BookLogix does not hold any ownership of the content of this book and is not liable in any way for the materials contained within. The views and opinions expressed in this book are the property of the Author/Copyright holder, and do not necessarily reflect those of BookLogix.

∞ This paper meets the requirements of ANSI/NISO Z39.48-1992 (Permanence of Paper)

070623

FIND YOUR VOICE
CURRICULUM EXECUTIVE SUMMARY
Pre-K to Third Grade

The "Find Your Voice" program provides an educational curriculum to equip children, pre-k to third grade, with the internal tools to prevent and combat abuse—emotional, physical, and sexual. The program offers lesson plans for each book in the Adventures of Gracie & Grant series. The curriculum provides a rubric-outlining lesson summary, skills introduced, and outcomes, which follows common core curriculum implemented in many school systems across the country. The curriculum reinforces the book themes in *Gracie Finds Her Voice*, *Grant Gets His Shield*, and *Gracie & Grant's Big Win* that educate children to have a powerful voice, personal boundaries, personal safety, and self-confidence.

Using traditional, innovative, and research-based methods, the Adventures of Gracie & Grant series subtly imparts empowerment through class-appropriate topics and lessons. The easy lesson plans allow the instructor to use natural conversation to facilitate the learning experience as the students read or follow along with the Dr. Seuss–style stories. The book series is comprised of colorful, entertaining, engaging, rhyming books and were specifically designed to maintain a child's innocence while educating them on the important principles of personal safety.

The Adventures of Gracie & Grant is destined to hold a place in the hearts of children who read them for generations.

Thank you for teaching the "Find Your Voice" curriculum, which strengthens valuable lessons of personal power, personal boundaries, and personal responsibility and safety, to help protect our children's innocence. If you are not able to purchase the Adventures of Gracie and Grant series to accompany the lessons, we have provided a complimentary PowerPoint to download on the QR Code:

CURRICULUM OVERVIEW

Gracie Finds Her Voice
Book Teaching Point: Personal Power

	Lesson Summary	Skills Introduced or Utilized	Outcomes
Lesson 1 *Gracie Finds Her Voice* (Approximately 40 minutes)	Harmful effects of secret keeping when a student steals and asks another student to keep it a secret.	*Critical-Thinking skills *Objective-Reasoning skills	Students will have understanding of motive. Students will have understanding of consequences of decisions.
Lesson 2 "Our Own Secrets" (Approximately 1.25 hours – Suggest two sessions)	Knowing the difference between surprises and secrets.	*Recall *Compare and Contrast	Students will be able to differentiate and act on knowledge of surprises and secrets.
Lesson 3 "Make Our Voices Heard" (Approximately 55 minutes)	Discovering that each person has a voice and can use it to protect themselves from anything that is harmful to them.	*Recall *Self-awareness *Self in the world	Students will be able to discern a potentially harmful motive and use their voice to help protect themselves.

Grant Gets His Shield
Book Teaching Point: Personal Boundaries

	Lesson Summary	Skills Introduced or Utilized	Outcomes
Lesson 1 *Grant Gets His Shield* (Approximately 45 minutes)	Setting personal boundaries with an overly affectionate great aunt who kisses and pinches.	*Self-awareness *Empathic problem-solving	Students will be able to communicate and set comfortable boundaries.
Lesson 2 "Role-Play" (Approximately 40 minutes)	Exposure to personal boundaries and practice through roleplay of positive responses to assert personal space.	*Self-awareness *Positive communication	Students will recognize and feel confident asserting their personal space.
Lesson 3 "Protecting Ourselves" (Approximately 40 minutes)	Character relation to model proper response when trying to protect themselves.	*Recall *Positive communication	Students will recognize and build courage asserting their personal space.
Lesson 4 "Being Courageous" (Approximately 30 minutes)	Character relation to model an abstract concept of courage.	*Recall *Empathy *Self-awareness	Students will be able to differentiate between fear and courage.

Gracie & Grant's Big Win
Book Teaching Point: Self-Confidence

	Lesson Summary	Skills Introduced or Utilized	Outcomes
Lesson 1 "Being Unique" (Approximately 30 minutes)	Using character modeling to identify perceived differences; self-awareness and uniqueness are taught.	*Communication *Self-awareness	Students will be able to identify and perpetuate some of their own unique abilities.
Lesson 2 "Wall of Compliments" (Approximately 33 minutes)	Using character modeling; empathy is taught through example.	*Empathy *Positive communication	Student will be able to recognize good qualities and communicate their observations.

Lesson Plan

Gracie Finds Her Voice

Lesson # 1: *Gracie Finds Her Voice*

Teacher's Overview

Lesson time: 40 minutes   Preparation time: 10 minutes

Lesson Summary

In this lesson, students will become introduced to Gracie and Grant through reading *Gracie Finds Her Voice*. They will start to think critically about the harmful effects of secret keeping.

Lesson Objectives

By the end of this lesson, students will be able to:
1. List all of the main characters in *Gracie Finds Her Voice*.
2. Describe who completed what actions in the story.
3. Explain when characters completed these actions.
4. Explain why characters completed their actions.
5. Describe how characters and their traits relate to major events and challenges.

Materials Provided	Materials Needed
Books (one for each child)	

Teacher Preparation	Room Setup
Ensure there are enough books (one for each child)	Have the room set up to facilitate group reading (preferably in a circle)

Part 1: Book Introduction (5 minutes)

Say: Today, we are going to start on an adventure with two very special friends, Gracie and Grant! Over this upcoming week, we will read about them both and get to learn some very important lessons. So, let's go ahead and each grab a book!

Teacher's note: Pass out one book to each student.

Say: The book is called *Gracie Finds Her Voice*. This is Gracie on the front cover. Where do you think her voice went? Did she lose it?

Teacher's note: Let a few students give their ideas

 Say: How do you think she will find her voice?

Teacher's note: Let a few students give their ideas

 Say: Let's go ahead and start reading the book to find out if you all are right!

Part 2: Reading *Gracie Finds Her Voice* **(20 minutes)**

Teacher's note: As the teacher reads the book, pause occasionally to ask questions to ensure comprehension. This can include the following comments, and feel free to add your own!

Little Gracie loved school
Every single, little bit.
She loved the playground most of all
And she loved to run around it.

Gracie Finds Her Voice

But she hit her toe on a rock
And fell and scraped her knee.
The teacher made her go inside
And have the nurse take a see.

A bandage and a lollipop
Had her feeling better fast.
But when she started back outside,
She heard a noise from her class!

She took a peek through the door
And saw her friend Grant inside!
He took a toy from the teacher's desk.
"Don't do that!" she cried.

Grant turned around quick,
And he looked really mad.
He was Gracie's friend, after all,
So it made her really sad.

Say: What is her friend, Grant, doing?

Listen for: Stealing a toy from his teacher.

Gracie Finds Her Voice

"Don't tell anyone, Gracie,"
Grant said, "or I will get in trouble!
This can be our little secret."
That idea made Gracie's tummy bubble.

They heard the whistle blow,
The class was on their way!
"Promise me, Gracie!"
"I promise," she heard herself say.

Say: Why is her tummy bubbling? Has anyone ever had that same feeling?

Listen for: She is nervous and does not like that her friend asked her to keep a secret.

That night, Gracie could not eat.
She felt sick and knew she should tell.
But she promised she wouldn't
And knew Grant would yell!

When she went up to her room
And crawled into her bed,
Her mommy came in
And patted her on the head.

Gracie Finds Her Voice

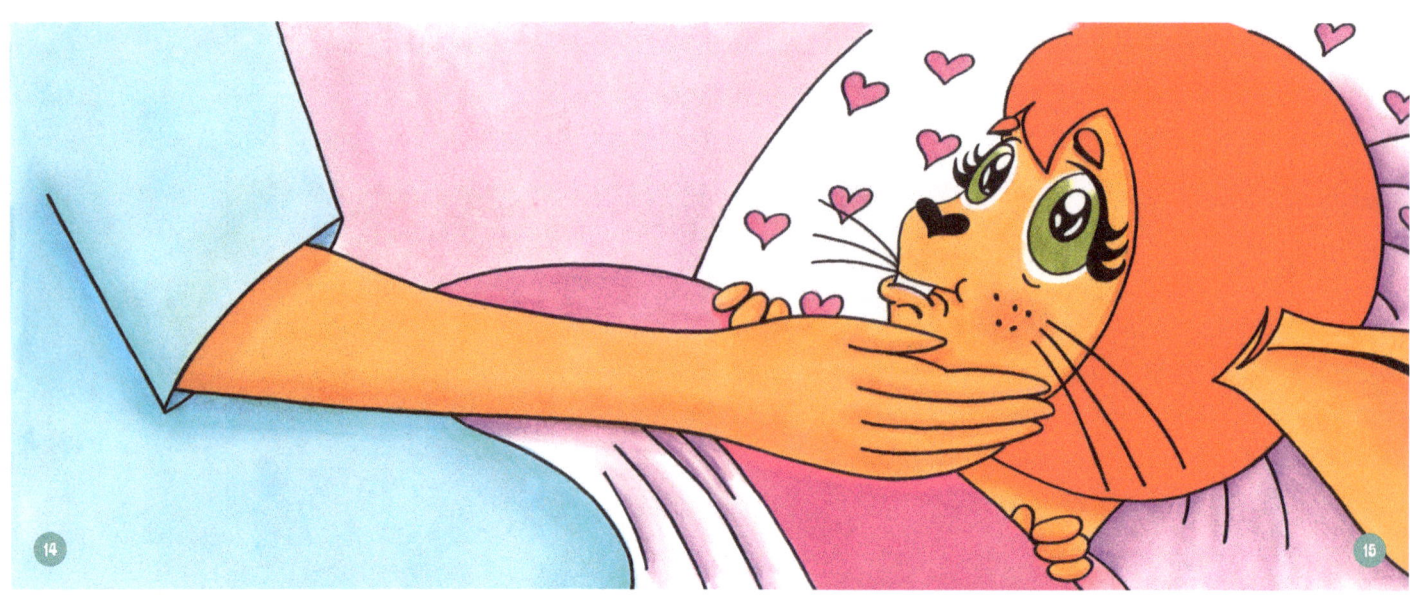

"What's wrong, Gracie?"
Her mother asked with worry.
"You can tell me anything,
And I'll help you in a hurry."

Gracie shook her little head
And bit her lip with fear.
"If you don't tell me what's going on,
I can't protect you, my dear."

Gracie opened up her mouth,
Her sweet little head fell.
"I saw a friend do something bad,
But I promised I would not tell."

"Secrets are never good,"
Her mother said, like she knew.
"They leave you feeling really bad,
And you get stuck in them, like glue."

Gracie Finds Her Voice

"So come on, Gracie, you can tell me.
When you say it, you will feel better."
But Gracie could not say a word.
No, she could not say a letter.

"Okay, Gracie. Maybe later,"
Her mother sadly said.
She stood up, turned out the light,
And tucked Gracie into bed.

Gracie tossed and turned,
She just could not fall asleep.
But soon enough, she nodded off,
And her sleep was very deep.

"Hey there, Gracie!"
Said a friendly voice she did not know.
She sat up and yawned
And opened her eyes real slow.

Gracie Finds Her Voice

A fuzzy, purple creature
Was sitting on the ground!
And giant colorful flowers
Were growing all around!

 **Say:** Where is Gracie?

"This place is awesome!"
Said Gracie with a smile.
It was the best she had felt
In quite a long while.

Listen for: She is having a dream.

"I know it is,"
Said the Fuzzy thing with a grin.
"And you can always come back,
If you do something for me again."

Say: Who is the fuzzy thing? What does he represent?

Listen for: He represents her secret.

"You see now, Gracie,
I'm the secret you've been keeping.
I'm not so bad now, am I?
As long as you stop speaking."

Say: What is he asking Gracie to do?

Listen for: He is asking her to stop speaking in order to keep the secret.

Gracie Finds Her Voice

His words were really sweet,
And he looked really nice,
But that last little part,
Turned Gracie's heart into ice.

"What do you mean stop speaking?"
She asked with a whimper.
The images around her started to shimmer.

"I mean, give up your voice,"
The creature said with a frown.
"Tell a lie if you have to,
Or just don't make a sound."

"I do not like that idea,"
Gracie said with fear.
The flowers and colors
All disappeared.

Say: Do you all think that she should listen to the creature?

Listen for: No, he wants her to lie.

Say: What do you think Gracie will do?

Listen for: Listen to the creature; speak out anyway.

Gracie Finds Her Voice

Dark clouds rolled in,
And the light went away.
The magical place
All turned to gray.

"I tried to play nice,"
The creature said as he grew.
"Now I will try mean!"
Gracie did not know
What to do!

The little fuzzy thing
Grew ten feet tall!
His teeth got really sharp,
But that was not all!

His eyes went dark red,
And his fur turned all black.
He grew nasty claws.
He was a monster,
And that is a fact!

Say: Did your answer change? What do you all think Gracie will do now?

Listen for: Listen to the creature; speak out anyway.

Gracie Finds Her Voice

But Gracie stood tall.
No she did not run.
She had been scared all day
But now she was done!

The big furry monster
Took a big monster leap.
And right on top of Gracie,
He fell in a heap.

But from inside the darkness,
A big "NO!" she screamed.
And the monster flew back
A hundred feet it seemed!

A new Gracie stood up,
All dressed for the fight.
She would never give up her voice,
Not when she knew what was right!

 Say: What did Gracie do? How did she fight back against the monster?

Listen for: She found her "NO!" voice!

Gracie Finds Her Voice

Her cape flew out behind her,
A big "V" glowed on her chest.
She brushed off her hands,
And she handled the rest.

"I will tell whoever I want!"
She yelled at the monster.
He shrunk down a size.
No, he could not beat her!

"I will tell my mom and dad,
And they will always believe me!
I will tell my teacher or my friends,
Even if it is not easy!"

"No matter what, I have my voice!
And you can never take it!
No, I'll use my weapon,
So be gone with you, secret!"

Say: What does Gracie mean by her "weapon"?

Listen for: Her weapon is her voice that she will use to tell the secret.

Gracie Finds Her Voice

And all the whole time,
The monster did shrink.
And with the last line,
He went with a wink!

Poof! He was gone,
And the colors all returned!
Gracie could not wait to wake
And use what she learned!

Her alarm clock went off,
And she shot out of bed.
She went straight to her mom,
And the whole truth she said.

Gracie's mom called the teacher,
Who then called up Grant,
Who gave back the toy,
Then to school they both went.

Gracie Finds Her Voice

"I'm really sorry, Gracie,"
Said Grant, looking ashamed,
"I put you in a bad spot.
Stealing isn't a game. . ."

"It's okay, Grant,"
Gracie said with a smile.
"Let me share what I learned!
And let's swing for a while."

Now use what you learned
From Gracie's adventure
To draw your secret you
Want to tell.

Break Time (3 minutes)

 Say: Everyone stand up and stretch! Let's take a three-minute break.

Part 3: Gracie's Secret (5 minutes)

 Say: In this book, Gracie's friend, Grant, asks her to keep a secret. Has anyone been asked to keep a secret before?

Teacher's note: Allow students to respond by raising their hands.

 Say: How did it feel when you were asked to keep a secret?

Listen for: Sad, nervous, stomach hurt, confused.

Review/Check for Knowledge (5 minutes)

 Say: Let's review what we learned about today while reading *Gracie Finds Her Voice*. Who are the characters in the book?

Listen for: Gracie, Grant, Gracie's mom, the fuzzy purple creature, Gracie and Grant's teacher.

 Say: What did Grant do, and what did he ask Gracie to do?

Listen for: Grant stole a toy from his teacher's desk, and he asked Gracie to keep a secret.

 Say: What happened to Gracie that night?

Listen for: She dreamed about a fuzzy, purple creature that told her to keep secrets, even if that meant lying. She defeated the purple creature by standing tall and using her voice.

 Say: After Gracie woke up, what did she do?

Listen for: She told her mom, who told their teacher.

 Say: How did Grant respond?

Listen for: Grant apologized.

Gracie Finds Her Voice

Next Class Preview (2 minutes)

Next class, we will talk more about secrets and how to fight them off!

Lesson # 2: Our Own Secrets

Teacher's Overview

Lesson time: 1 hour, 15 minutes   Preparation time: 15 minutes

Lesson Summary

In this lesson, students will think critically about a time in their lives when they were asked to keep a secret. They will either demonstrate through drawing, how they fought off that secret or what they could have done to fight off that secret. They also will learn the difference between surprises and secrets. Students will wrap a gift to show that surprises are fun and make you feel happy.

Lesson Objectives

By the end of this lesson, students will be able to:
1. Define "secret" in their own words.
2. Describe, through drawing, how they have fought off a secret.
3. Describe the difference between secrets and surprises.

Materials Provided	Materials Needed
Gracie Finds Her Voice books for reference	Copy paper Crayons, colored pencils, markers Wrapping paper Small Box Tape

16

Gracie Finds Her Voice

Teacher Preparation	Room Setup
Collect enough materials for all students. Go ahead and cut wrapping paper to save time.	The students will need tables and chairs to do their drawings and wrap their boxes.

Part 1: What is a Secret? (20 minutes)

Say: Who can tell me about the story, *Gracie Finds Her Voice*, that we read yesterday? What happened between Gracie and Grant?

Listen for: Grant asked Gracie to keep a secret. After she felt bad about keeping the secret, Gracie had to stand tall against her secret to overcome it.

Say: Keeping a secret is never a good idea. Secrets make our tummy hurt because we know we are hiding something that we should not hide. Think about what the word "secret" means to you. I'm going to pass out paper and markers to you all, and I want you all to create a drawing that represents "secrets" to you. It could be helpful to think about a time that someone has told you to keep a secret or maybe a secret that you have.

Teacher's note: Give the students five to ten minutes to create their drawing.

Say: Is there anyone who would like to share their drawing with the group?

Teacher's note: Allow anyone to share who wants to share, depending on time

Say: When coming up with your drawing, what kinds of things did you think about? How do you define "secret"?

Teacher's note: Get two to three definitions from students.

Part 2: Fighting off a Secret (15 minutes)

Say: Has anyone had to fight off a secret like Gracie did? How did you all fight it off?

Teacher's note: Get two to three responses from students.

Gracie Finds Her Voice

 Say: Let's all think about a time that someone asked you to keep a secret. Did you fight it off and share the secret with someone you trust? If you didn't, what could you have done to fight it off? Once you have thought about that secret, draw a picture representing you fighting off a secret.

Teacher's note: Pass out a new sheet of paper to each student.

 Say: Is there anyone who would like to share their drawing with the group?

Break Time (3 minutes)

 Say: Everyone stand up and stretch! Let's take a three-minute break.

Part 3: Secrets Conceal, Surprises Reveal (30 minutes)

Say: Raise your hand if you have ever gone to a birthday party or a surprise party. Wasn't it a lot of fun? If it was a surprise party, you couldn't tell the person you were going to surprise, could you? Did it make your tummy hurt to not tell that person?

Listen for: Going to a birthday party or a surprise party is fun. The person you want to surprise will be so happy. It doesn't make my tummy hurt to keep a surprise because it is good for the other person.

Say: Surprises are fun because they make someone feel good and happy. It is hard to keep a surprise a secret because you know it will make the other person so happy! Secrets are not fun because they hide the truth and could hurt someone. There is a difference in secrets and surprises. Secrets do not make you feel happy while surprises make you feel happy!

If you see another student push a child on the playground, and don't tell a grown-up, is that a surprise or a secret? How do you know?

Listen for: It's a secret because it was not nice for the student to push the child. It would make my tummy hurt if I did not tell a grown-up. The child may have gotten hurt.

Say: You buy a gift for your friend to give her on her birthday. Is that a surprise or a secret? How do you know?

Listen for: It is a surprise because it is a gift and will make my friend happy.

Say: To help you remember that surprises are good things that you want to share, we are going to wrap a gift. You have your boxes on your desk. Pick out a piece of wrapping paper from your table to wrap your box.

Teacher's note: Give the students twenty to twenty-five minutes to wrap their gifts

Review/Check for Knowledge (5 minutes)

Say: Fantastic work today, everyone! Let's review what we did today. First, who can give their own definition of a "secret"?

Listen for: A secret is something that someone makes you keep and not tell anyone. It could be something bad that the other person did.

Say: Great! Who can tell me what a "surprise" is?

Listen for: A surprise is something that is fun and makes you feel happy or excited.

Lesson # 3: Make Our Voices Heard

Teacher's Overview

Lesson time: 55 minutes   Preparation time: 10 minutes

Lesson Summary
In this lesson, students will learn the importance of using their voices. Students will learn to empower themselves by telling people "NO!" and create small microphones to project their voices.

Lesson Objectives

By the end of this lesson, students will be able to:
1. Redefine the meaning of a secret.
2. Discuss the importance of using our voice to say "NO!"
3. Create microphones to project voices.

Materials Provided	Materials Needed
Gracie Finds Her Voice books for reference	Toilet paper tube (one per student) Styrofoam ball (one per student) Construction paper Glitter, stickers, other materials White glue Hot glue gun Scissors

Gracie Finds Her Voice

Teacher Preparation	Room Setup
Collect enough materials for all students.	The students will need tables and chairs to create their microphones.

Part 1: What Is a Secret? (10 minutes)

 Say: Who can tell me about the story, *Gracie Finds Her Voice*, that we read yesterday? What happened between Gracie and Grant?

Listen for: Grant asked Gracie to keep a secret. After she felt bad about keeping the secret, Gracie had to stand tall against her secret to overcome it.

Say: Yesterday, we talked about what a "secret" is. Can anybody tell me what we learned?

Teacher's note: Call on one or two students to respond.

Say: That's right! A secret is something that someone makes you keep and not tell anyone. It could be something bad that the other person did. Keeping a secret is never a good idea. They make us feel strange because we know we are hiding something. Yesterday, we also made drawings that represented secrets to us.

Teacher's note: Open the book to page 28 and read the story to page 37.

Part 2: "NO!" voice (40 minutes)

 Say: Who remembers what Gracie had to do to defeat the fuzzy, purple creature?

Listen for: She stood tall and screamed "NO!" She yelled at the monster that she would tell whoever she wants, knowing that her parents and teacher would believe her.

Say: We want to be able to use our "NO!" voices too and make sure they are loud and strong! If anyone ever asks us to keep a secret or if anyone ever does anything that makes us uncomfortable or scared, the thing to do is:
- Yell "NO!"
- Run away
- Tell someone

So what do we need to do if someone asks us to keep a secret or makes us uncomfortable or scared? All together!

Listen for (in unison):
- Yell "NO!"
- Run away
- Tell someone

Say: In order for our "NO!" voices to be heard, we need to say it loud and proud! So, today, we're going to make our "NO!" voice microphones! Microphones help us protect our voices and be heard loudly.

Say: Each of you is going to take the supplies I give you to make your microphones and decorate them. Everyone will take a toilet paper tube—that's the handle—plus a Styrofoam ball. We'll cover the toilet paper tube by gluing on construction paper—any color you want—and we'll glue tin foil on the Styrofoam ball. Once you've done that and decorated your microphone handle however you want, call me over, and I'll help you glue the Styrofoam ball to the handle. Are there any questions?

Teacher's note: Give the students twenty to twenty-five minutes to decorate their microphones.

Say: Let's practice using our "NO!" voices! When I ask you to keep a secret, let's all yell "NO!" into our microphones! Ready?

"I know you saw me steal from a teacher, but let's just keep that between the two of us. It will be our secret.

(Students will yell "NO!" into their microphones.)

Awesome work! And can someone tell me what you would do after you yelled "NO!"

Listen for: Run away and tell someone

Review/Check for Knowledge (5 minutes)

Say: Good job, everyone! Let's review what we did today. If someone asks us to keep a secret—or if someone does something that makes us feel scared or uncomfortable—what do we do?

Listen for:
- Yell "NO!"
- Run away
- Tell someone

Lesson Plan

Grant Gets His Shield

Lesson # 1: *Grant Gets His Shield*

Teacher's Overview

Lesson time: 45 minutes   Preparation time: 10 minutes

> **Lesson Summary**
> In this lesson, students will learn about personal boundaries. Through Grant's experience with his great aunt Ruth and her pinches and kisses that make him feel uncomfortable, students will learn how to communicate and set comfortable boundaries.

Lesson Objectives

By the end of this lesson, students will be able to:
1. Identify what made Grant feel uncomfortable about his Great Aunt Ruth.
2. Identify what Grant did to resolve the problem.
3. Make a list of trusted adults to talk to when someone makes them feel uncomfortable.

Materials Provided	Materials Needed
Books (one for each student)	Copies of activity sheet (one for each student)

Teacher Preparation	Room Setup
Review book and activity beforehand	Have the room set up to facilitate group reading (preferably in a circle)

Part 1: What Is a Secret? (10 minutes)

Say: In our last book, we read about Gracie and how she found her voice. Today, we are going to read about her friend Grant. We met Grant in the story, *Gracie Finds Her Voice*.

Teacher's note: Pass out one book to each student.

Say: The book is called *Grant Gets His Shield*. Can anyone tell me what a shield is?

Grant Gets His Shield

> **Teacher's note:** Let a few students give their ideas.

 Say: What does a shield look like? What is a shield used for?

> **Teacher's note:** Let a few students giver their ideas. Be sure students know that a shield is used for protection.

 Say: Let's go ahead and start reading the book to find out how Grant gets his shield.

Part 2: Reading *Grant Gets His Shield* **(20 minutes)**

> **Teacher's note:** As the teacher reads the book, pause occasionally to ask questions to ensure comprehension. This can include the following comments, and feel free to add your own!

Grant just got out for the summer,
And was riding in the back of the car.
They were on their way to Grandma's house.
Thank goodness it wasn't far.

Grant Gets His Shield

His grandma was so wacky.
Together they did lots of fun things.
Last year they went on a rollercoaster.
He couldn't wait for what this visit would bring!

But as they neared her house,
He knew that it wouldn't be the same.
There was another car outside,
This time another visitor came.

Who could it be?
Who was inside?
He thought this time would be special.
Who was Granny sitting beside?

Grant's grandma introduced her.
For the first time, Grant met Great Aunt Ruth.
She was short and she was round,
With slobbery lips and missing a tooth!

Grant Gets His Shield

Grant's grandma tickled him,
Which made him laugh and grin,
But then, Aunt Ruth neared
And she didn't even ask him!

 Say: Looking at the picture of Grant, what do you think he is feeling? Why?

She planted a slobbery kiss
Right smack on his cheek
And pinched with a pinch
That would hurt for a week!

Listen for: He looks scared because he never met this aunt before and she is getting too close to him.

She wasn't all that bad,
But sat down by him with a plop.
She just kept kissing and pinching
How could he tell her to stop?

 Say: What did Grant's great aunt Ruth do? How do you think it made him feel?

The visit didn't last long,
His dad got a big call.
He was sad they had to leave,
But he hoped for a better visit in the fall.

Listen for: She gave him a slobbery kiss and pinched his cheeks. It hurt and he didn't like it. He wants her to stop.

Grant Gets His Shield

"Aunt Ruth is coming to visit."
When Grant heard, he just frowned.
He would never have any fun
If Great Aunt Ruth was around.

Grant didn't know what to do!
So when they pulled up to the house,
He called his best friend,
One really smart mouse!

Say: Who do you think Grant will call? Who do you talk to when you do not know what to do?

Listen for: Gracie. Someone that I trust, a parent, a friend, etc. . . . Let a few students respond and move on.

"Gracie!" he said,
With the phone to his ear,
"Great Aunt Ruth's on her way,
And she fills me with fear!"

"Oh no!" Gracie said,
"What happened on your trip?"
"I can't explain right now,
Just get over here quick!"

Grant Gets His Shield

Quick as a flash,
Gracie was at his front door.
Grant knew he could count on her,
For a best friend he couldn't ask for more.

"Her kisses are slobbery
And her pinches are rude,
But she seems really nice.
I just don't know what to do?"

"Well, remember that time
When you stole from the class,
I learned my 'NO!'
Maybe you could try that."

So they wandered outside
And were playing a game.
Their imaginations took over
And soon their world changed.

 Say: Do you think Gracie's suggestion of using his "NO voice" will work?

Listen for: Let a few students respond.

Grant Gets His Shield

Gracie smiled with joy
For she knew where they were.
It was the place she once dreamed.
They were in for a whirl.

 Say: Why do you think Gracie felt something was not right?

She was glad to see
She was dressed for a fight.
But she could tell right away,
Something just wasn't right.

Listen for: Gracie is ready with her powers for a fight but Grant is not.

"What's that?" Grant shouted
As he pointed to a hill.
Hundreds of crabs appeared,
And they were not standing still!

 Say: Why do the crabs have big lips and pinchers of steel?

They had puffy lips
And pinchers of steel.
They looked at Grant and Gracie
Like the friends were their meal.

Listen for: Because he is afraid of his great aunt Ruth's big slobbery kisses and her rude pinches.

Grant Gets His Shield

As the crabs rushed toward the friends,
Grant was scared, he couldn't move.
But Gracie leapt into action,
She was right in her groove.

She shouted her "NO!"
But the crabs did not stop.
They kept getting closer,
And soon they were on top.

"Grant, help!" Gracie cried,
But he was still filled with fear.
He didn't have any power,
And he ran when they neared.

He escaped from the crabs,
But had left Gracie all alone.
He felt like the biggest coward,
He wished it was courage he'd shown.

Grant Gets His Shield

He took a deep breath.
He knew he had to go back.
He was done being scared,
He was going on the attack.

Grant rushed to the crabs,
And they pinched him so hard.
He held out his fists
And he played his last card.

He imagined a great shield
To bash the crabs away.
It formed in his hands
And shot out a great ray.

The light banished the crabs
From their land of play.
Gracie was safe from the pinchers,
Grant had saved the day!

Grant Gets His Shield

Gracie ran and hugged her friend.
"I thought those crabs had won!
How did you beat them?
I thought you had run?"

"I did run, Gracie,
I didn't know what to do.
Your 'NO' didn't work,
I thought I would fail too."

"But after I ran,
I felt like such a coward.
I knew I had to come back,
So I got my own power."

Grant's shield stood strong.
"It keeps people out of my zone.
I pick who I let in,
I choose all on my own."

Say: What does Grant's shield do for him?

Listen for: Keeps people out of his comfort zone.

Grant Gets His Shield

"And when Great Aunt Ruth comes to town,
I know just what to do.
I'll sit her right down
And I'll tell her the truth."

Grant's mom yelled, "Dinnertime!"
And Gracie had to go too.
And with a blink of an eye,
Their dreamland vanished from view.

A couple days later,
Great Aunt Ruth was on her way.
Grant had been thinking and thinking
And knew just what to say.

So when she pulled up
And got out of her car,
She leaned in to pinch him
But didn't get very far.

Grant Gets His Shield

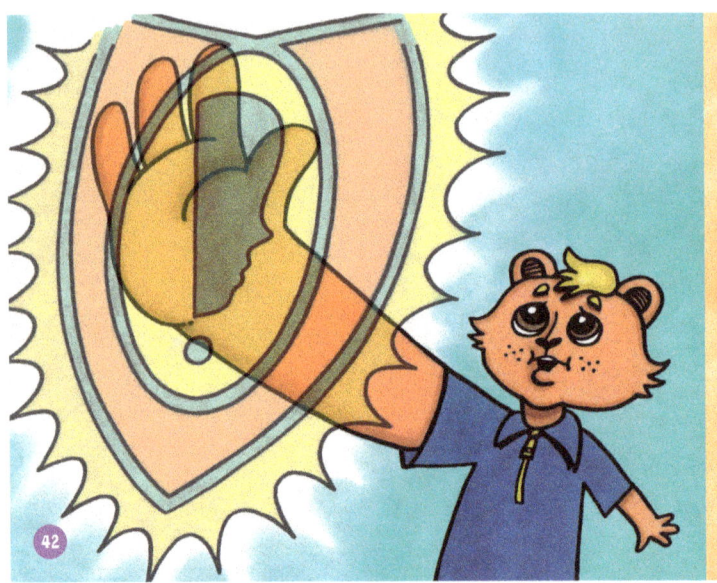

Grant held out his hand
And said, "Aunt Ruth, stop!
I know you don't mean to
But your pinches hurt a lot!"

"Your kisses are nice
But sometimes they slobber.
It sticks in my fur
And that's a real bother."

"Its only the second time we've met,
So how about for now,
We stick to high fives
Or maybe a fist pound?"

"I'm sorry, little buddy,
I didn't mean to get in your space.
We can get to know each other more,
And sorry about pinching your face."

Grant Gets His Shield

And after that day,
Grant and Great Aunt Ruth
Got along like best buds,
And that's the truth.

 Say: How does Grant feel after he told Great Aunt Ruth the truth about her kisses and pinches?

 Listen for: He felt better about the situation. He and Great Aunt Ruth were able to get along after he told her the truth.

Now use what you have learned from Grant's adventure to share if anyone makes you feel uncomfortable or afraid. You can draw a picture here if you want.

Grant Gets His Shield

Part 3: Grant's Shield (5 minutes)

 Say: In this book, Grant feels uncomfortable when his great aunt Ruth gives him slobbery kisses and painful pinches on the cheeks. At first, Grant doesn't know what to do. Has anyone felt uncomfortable around someone you just met?

Teacher's note: Allow students to respond by raising their hands.

 Say: How did it feel when you were around them?

Listen for: Nervous, scared, etc. . . .

Say: Grant used his shield to find courage to tell Great Aunt Ruth the truth about her slobbery kisses and rude pinches. What can you do when you feel uncomfortable around someone?

Listen for: Tell a parent, trusted adult, or friend.

Say: I want you to think of four people you can go to when you feel uncomfortable.

Activity (15 minutes)

On the activity sheet, draw four people you can go to for help when you feel uncomfortable.

Grant Gets His Shield

Lesson 1 Activity Sheet: Draw four people you can go to for help.

Grant Gets His Shield

Lesson # 2: Role-Play

Teacher's Overview

Lesson time: 40 minutes   Preparation time: 10 minutes

> ### Lesson Summary
> In this lesson, students will learn about personal boundaries. Students will role-play and practice what to say when someone makes them feel uncomfortable.

Lesson Objectives

By the end of this lesson, students will be able to:
1. Understand personal boundaries.
2. Confidently respond when someone has crossed into their personal space.
3. Learn about our own personal boundary.

Materials Provided	Materials Needed
Grant Gets His Shield (for reference) Role-playing scenarios	Hula-Hoop Blank copy paper Crayons

Teacher Preparation	Room Setup
Review scenarios and have one hula-hoop to role-play. Have copy paper and crayons ready for drawing activity.	Open space for role-play activity. Desks or tables for drawing activity.

Part 1: Intro to Role-Play (5 minutes)

Say: Who can tell me about the story, *Grant Gets His Shield*, that we read yesterday? What happened with Grant?

Listen for: Grant felt uncomfortable with his great aunt Ruth's slobbery kisses and rude pinches. He found confidence to tell her the truth about how it made him feel.

Grant Gets His Shield

Say: This was the first time he met his great aunt Ruth. She was a stranger to Grant. When you meet someone for the first time, how do you usually greet them?

Listen for: With a handshake or a wave.

Say: Grant felt so uncomfortable because Great Aunt Ruth crossed into his personal space. Does anyone know what I mean by "personal space"?

Listen for: When someone is too close to you and makes you feel uncomfortable.

Say: I am standing in a Hula-Hoop. If someone comes inside my Hula-Hoop, that means they have crossed into my personal space.

Say: Today, we are going to act out different scenarios and practice what to say if we find ourselves in a similar situation as Grant. Mrs./Mr. (Insert Name) and I will act out a few for you and then you will be able to do the same. If someone does not listen to your voice, tell one of your four safe people.

Part 2: Role-Playing Activity (20 minutes)

Say: The Hula-Hoop that you see me standing in is my personal space. Pay attention to how I respond when Mrs./Mr. (Insert Name) tries to cross into my personal space. It is okay to tell someone when they have crossed into your personal space. Remember, if someone does not listen to your voice, tell one of your four safe people.

Teacher's note: Teachers act out a few scenarios and show when someone is too close. Then have students act out the scenarios (with help, if needed). Students should repeat scenarios until they feel confident in their responses.

Say: Everyone did a great job role-playing. Let's have a seat so we can get ready for our next activity. Remember, if your response does not work, tell one of your four safe people.

Grant Gets His Shield

Role-Playing Scenario Cards

Scenario 1: Your mother's long-time friend comes over and wants you to sit in her lap.

Respond: "No, thank you. I will sit beside my mommy."

Scenario 2: Your cousin comes over to play and tickles you too much.

Respond: "Please do not tickle me anymore. I do not like it. How about we high-five?"

Scenario 3: Your sibling's friend comes over and wants to play in your room.

Respond: "Please do not play in my room. How about we play outside instead?"

Scenario 4: You meet someone new in your classroom and they want to give you a hug.

Respond: "How about we shake hands, fist bump, or high five for now?"

Scenario 5: You go over to a friend's house and their sibling sits too close to you.

Respond: "Please scoot over a little. I need some more room."

Scenario 6:

Respond:

Part 2: Drawing (10 minutes)

Say: Now, use what you have learned from Grant's adventure to share if anyone makes you feel unsafe or afraid. You can draw your picture on the last page of the book or on a sheet of paper. There is a sad face on one side. Draw your picture here if you have felt unsafe or afraid. If you have not felt this way, draw a picture on the side with a happy face.

Teacher's note: Give students time to finish drawings and return to the teacher.

Review/Check for Knowledge (5 minutes)

Say: Fantastic work today, everyone! Let's review what we did today. First, who can tell me what personal space is?

Listen for: The space around you that makes you feel comfortable. When someone gets into your personal space, you feel uncomfortable.

Say: Is it okay to tell someone when they have crossed into your personal space?

Listen for: Yes. We can respond confidently in many different ways. We have the right and responsibility to protect our personal space.

Grant Gets His Shield

Grant Gets His Shield

Grant Gets His Shield

Lesson # 3: Protecting Ourselves

Teacher's Overview

Lesson time: 40 minutes   Preparation time: 10 minutes

> **Lesson Summary**
> In this lesson, students will learn how to communicate and set comfortable boundaries by demonstrating how to protect themselves in uncomfortable situations.

Lesson Objectives

By the end of this lesson, students will be able to:
1. Identify how Grant was able to protect himself in the story *Grant Gets His Shield*.
2. Review personal boundaries.
3. Protect themselves in uncomfortable situations.

Materials Provided	Materials Needed
Grant Gets His Shield (for reference)	Copies of cut-out shield Markets, crayons, pencils Chart paper

Teacher Preparation	Room Setup
Grant Gets His Shield (for reference) Copies of shield activity sheet	Have room set up to facilitate group reading (preferably in a circle.)

Part 1: Book Summary (10 minutes)

Say: In our last lesson, we read about how Grant got his shield. We learned that he got the courage to tell his great aunt Ruth how her kisses and pinches made him feel uncomfortable.

Teacher's note: Hold up the front of the book for students to see.

Grant Gets His Shield

 Say: Do you remember what we discussed? What can you do when you feel uncomfortable around someone?

Teacher's note: Teacher uses a marker to write ideas on chart paper.

 Say: That's right! We can . . . (teacher reads a few of student responses.) Let's review what happened to Grant in the beginning of the story.

Teacher's note: Show students the book. Quickly summarize pages 1–20, stopping on pages to discuss events of the book.

 Say: (Refer to page 16) Remember, in the story, how Grant was nervous about Great Aunt Ruth's second visit? He didn't know what to do so he called his friend Gracie. Yesterday, we used the Hula-Hoops to show others where our personal boundaries are around our body. Today we will discuss how Grant protected his personal boundaries in the story. (Begin reading on page 21.)

Part 2: Reading *Grant Gets His Shield* (20 minutes)

So they wandered outside
And were playing a game.
Their imaginations took over
And soon their world changed.

Gracie smiled with joy
For she knew where they were.
It was the place she once dreamed.
They were in for a whirl.

She was glad to see
She was dressed for a fight.
But she could tell right away,
Something just wasn't right.

"What's that?" Grant shouted
As he pointed to a hill.
Hundreds of crabs appeared,
And they were not standing still!

They had puffy lips
And pinchers of steel.
They looked at Grant and Gracie
Like the friends were their meal.

 Say: Looking at the picture, what do you think he is feeling? Why?

Listen for: He looks scared because he sees them coming and doesn't know what to do.

As the crabs rushed toward the friends,
Grant was scared, he couldn't move.
But Gracie leapt into action,
She was right in her groove.

She shouted her "NO!"
But the crabs did not stop.
They kept getting closer,
And soon they were on top.

 Say: What happened after Gracie tried using her "no voice"? How do you think it made her feel? Who did she need help from?

Listen for: The crabs got closer and closer. She needed Grant to help her.

"Grant, help!" Gracie cried,
But he was still filled with fear.
He didn't have any power,
And he ran when they neared.

Grant Gets His Shield

He escaped from the crabs,
But had left Gracie all alone.
He felt like the biggest coward,
He wished it was courage he'd shown.

He took a deep breath.
He knew he had to go back.
He was done being scared,
He was going on the attack.

 Say: What does that mean, "going on the attack"? How was Grant feeling and what was he going to do next?

Listen for: He wants to fight them, he is standing up for himself or wanting to use his voice.

Grant rushed to the crabs,
And they pinched him so hard.
He held out his fists
And he played his last card.

He imagined a great shield
To bash the crabs away.
It formed in his hands
And shot out a great ray.

The light banished the crabs
From their land of play.
Gracie was safe from the pinchers,
Grant had saved the day!

Gracie ran and hugged her friend.
"I thought those crabs had won!
How did you beat them?
I thought you had run?"

"I did run, Gracie,
I didn't know what to do.
Your 'NO' didn't work,
I thought I would fail too."

"But after I ran,
I felt like such a coward.
I knew I had to come back,
So I got my own power."

Grant's shield stood strong.
"It keeps people out of my zone.
I pick who I let in,
I choose all on my own."

 Say: So, how did Grant finally get rid of the giant crabs?

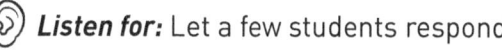

Listen for: Let a few students respond.

 Say: What does Grant's shield do for him? How does it keep him safe?

 Listen for: Keeps people/things out of his personal space.

 Say: Right. The shield also protects Grant from anything or anyone getting into his personal space. Today, we are going to be making our own personal shields. We can use them if we are ever in an uncomfortable situation and are unable to use our voices.

Grant Gets His Shield

Part 3: Making Our Own Shield (10 minutes)

 Say: In this book, Grant feels uncomfortable when the crabs are coming after him, but he is unable to use his voice. Sometimes, we can use our hands or create a physical shield to keep people or things out of our personal space.

Teacher's note: Show students a model of a premade shield.

 Say: This is my shield that I use to keep people out of my personal space. (Ask a student to come up and try to touch you without permission. First, tell them to stop and when they don't, hold up the shield to block the student from touching you. Ask students what word they think of when they see a red light. What do cars do at a red light? Explain that is how the shield works. It tells others to stop what they are doing so that we don't feel uncomfortable.)

 Say: How did the shield help me when (student) tried to touch me?

Listen for: It kept them from touching you.

 Say: That's right! Grant used his shield to fight the crabs and in the end, he found the courage to tell Great Aunt Ruth the truth about her slobbery kisses and rude pinches.

So what can we do or say when someone crosses into our personal space?

Listen for: We can respond by using our voice or by using physical ways to protect our personal space.

Activity (15 minutes)

Teacher will pass out shields, pencils, and markers. Students will create their own shields like the one Grant had in the story. (Shields can be various colors as well.) Students can write words like "stop" and "no" on their shields or other phrases that will help them remember the purpose of the shield. Have two to three students share if time permits. Students can take them home and use them to discuss what they learned with family or friends.

Grant Gets His Shield

49

Grant Gets His Shield

Lesson # 4: Being Courageous

Teacher's Overview

Lesson time: 30 minutes   Preparation time: 10 minutes

Lesson Summary
In this lesson, students will learn what it means to be courageous. Students will reflect on their own lives and think about a time when they had to overcome fear.

Lesson Objectives

By the end of this lesson, students will be able to:
1. Define "courageous."
2. Identify how Grant was able to be courageous in the story.
3. Share about a time when fear had to be overcome.

Materials Provided	Materials Needed
Books (one for each student)	Copies of activity sheet (one for each student) Crayons and/or markers

Teacher Preparation	Room Setup
Ensure there are enough books for each student. Copies of activity sheet.	Have room set up to facilitate group reading (preferably in a circle)

Part 1: Book Introduction (5 minutes)

 Say: In our last book, we read about Grant and how he was able to protect himself from his great aunt Ruth.

Teacher's note: Pass out one book to each student.

Grant Gets His Shield

 Say: Does anyone remember how Grant was able to keep himself safe? What did he need to protect?

Teacher's note: Let a few students give their responses.

 Say: That's right! He wanted to protect his personal space. Remember when we used Hula-Hoops to show us where our personal space was? Our personal space is important; it lets us know when someone is too close to us, and if they are making us uncomfortable. What does a shield look like and what do we use it for?

Teacher's note: Let a few students giver their ideas.

 Say: Good. Grant used the shield in the story to protect himself from the crabs. Sometimes we can use shields to keep people from touching us. Today, we are going to talk about how to be courageous when we are scared. Does anyone know what the word "courageous" means?

 Listen for: It means he was brave.

 Say: Sometimes we have to do things that seem scary so we don't want to do them. This is when we have to be courageous or brave if we want to do those things. These things are very important, so we have to push past our fear to do them. Let's read in the story where Grant was courageous.

Part 2: Reading *Grant Gets His Shield* **(15 minutes)**

Say: The Hula-Hoop you see me standing in is my personal space. Pay attention to how I respond when Mrs./Mr. (Insert Name) tries to cross into my personal space. It is okay to tell someone when they have crossed into your personal space. Remember, if someone does not listen to your voice, tell one of your four safe people.

Teacher's note: As the teacher reads the book, stop and ask comprehensive questions to check for students understanding. Discuss how Grant is hiding from the crabs.

He escaped from the crabs,
But had left Gracie all alone.
He felt like the biggest coward,
He wished it was courage he'd shown.

He took a deep breath.
He knew he had to go back.
He was done being scared,
He was going on the attack.

Grant rushed to the crabs,
And they pinched him so hard.
He held out his fists
And he played his last card.

He imagined a great shield
To bash the crabs away.
It formed in his hands
And shot out a great ray.

The light banished the crabs
From their land of play.
Gracie was safe from the pinchers,
Grant had saved the day!

Gracie ran and hugged her friend.
"I thought those crabs had won!
How did you beat them?
I thought you had run?"

"I did run, Gracie,
I didn't know what to do.
Your 'NO' didn't work,
I thought I would fail too."

"But after I ran,
I felt like such a coward.
I knew I had to come back,
So I got my own power."

Grant's shield stood strong.
"It keeps people out of my zone.
I pick who I let in,
I choose all on my own."

 Say: How was Grant courageous against the crabs? Do you think he was still scared? Why did he need to do it?

Listen for: He used his shield to get the crabs to go away. He was scared, but he did it anyway.

 Say: Great! Now listen and see if Grant was courageous when he saw his great aunt Ruth.

A couple days later,
Great Aunt Ruth was on her way.
Grant had been thinking and thinking
And knew just what to say.

So when she pulled up
And got out of her car,
She leaned in to pinch him
But didn't get very far.

Grant held out his hand
And said, "Aunt Ruth, stop!
I know you don't mean to
But your pinches hurt a lot!"

"Your kisses are nice
But sometimes they slobber.
It sticks in my fur
And that's a real bother."

"Its only the second time we've met,
So how about for now,
We stick to high fives
Or maybe a fist pound?"

"I'm sorry, little buddy,
I didn't mean to get in your space.
We can get to know each other more,
And sorry about pinching your face."

 Say: How did Grant show courage with his great aunt Ruth? How do you think it made him feel?

Listen for: He told her how he felt. He felt good after.

Grant Gets His Shield

Part 3: Stories of Courage (10 minutes)

 Say: In this book, Grant gets scared but has to overcome his fears. I remember this time when I was really scared to . . . (tell a story of when you overcame fear. Tell them how you were scared but it was important that you be courageous in the situation. Have students turn and talk about a time that they were courageous.)

Teacher's note: Allow students to sit with each other (crisscross, sitting in front of each other) and whisper about a specific time they were courageous..

 Say: How did it feel when you had to be courageous like Grant? Does someone want to share?

 Listen for: Allow one or two students to share.

Say: Great! Now I want you to think about how you would tell that story to a friend. Pretend you are telling a story and you need to think of how to tell the story from beginning to end. Today, you are going to be writing about a time you had to be brave like Grant.

Activity (15 minutes)

On the activity sheet, have students think of one story they can write about. If they can't write the story, have them draw pictures in each box. If time permits, have one or two students share.

Check for understanding: Review the word "courageous" with students. Have them summarize how Grant was courageous in the story.

Grant Gets His Shield

Being Courageous!

I was courageous when . . . _____

_____

_____

_____

_____

I was courageous when . . .

Lesson Plan

Gracie & Grant's Big Win

Gracie & Grant's Big Win

Lesson # 1: Being Unique

Teacher's Overview

Lesson time: 30 minutes   Preparation time: 15 minutes

Lesson Summary

In this lesson, students will understand what it means to be unique. Students will also learn how being unique gives us confidence to be who we are.

Lesson Objectives

By the end of this lesson, students will be able to:
1. Understand what it means to be unique.
2. Understand what it means to be confident in who you are and to like yourself for being Unique.

Materials Provided	Materials Needed
Gracie & Grant's Big Win book	Markers and/or crayons Colored paper Stickers, glue, other craft items Puzzle-piece cutouts

Teacher Preparation	Room Setup
Prepare one puzzle piece for each child (pre-cut and glue to construction paper). Teacher-made puzzle piece as an example.	Kids sitting on the carpet. Desks or table for puzzle activity.

Part 1: What Does It Mean to Be Unique? (20 minutes)

Teacher's note: Teacher begins by inviting students to the carpet for the read aloud.

Say: Have you ever felt like you were different? Well today we are going to read a story called *Gracie & Grant's Big Win*. This is a story about how Gracie and Grant learn to accept who they are despite being different.

Teacher's note: Read the book to students. Stop along the way to clarify and answer questions.

Teacher will read the following part:

"Gracie," Grant said,
As he brushed off the blow,
"I think your ears are cool,
And I just like when they show."

"Really?" Gracie asked.
Then she smiled bright!
"I wish I had big feet,
You can kick a ball out of sight!"

After reading the story, teacher will continue.

Early one Monday morning,
Our friends get ready for class.
They're running a bit late,
So they better move fast!

Gracie & Grant's Big Win

"Grant!" his father yelled
From the very last stair.
Grant had slept way too late!
He rushed and tripped on a chair!

"My feet are too big,"
He thought with a frown.
He ran to his dad
And stumbled all the way down.

Gracie threw her headband
And held back her tears.
Her new, favorite one
Wouldn't fit over her ears!

"They're floppy and weird,"
She muttered real sad.
She hopped in her mom's car,
Thinking her ears really looked bad.

Math and science were over,
And recess time came.
The friends slouched to the playground,
Both feeling real lame.

"Hey, Gracie," Grant said,
Where did your headband go?
You always wear one.
Now your ears really show."

And just as he finished,
Grant tripped over his own feet!
Grant felt like crying,
It had happened all week!

"Ha-ha," Gracie laughed,
You can barely even walk.
You're feet are so huge,
You shouldn't be the one to talk!"

Grant stood up slowly
And held back his tears.
He was so mad at Gracie he yelled
"You have ugly ears!"

Gracie started to cry,
And ran all the way home.
Grant wandered off too,
He just felt like being alone.

Gracie sat on the swings
That stood behind her house.
"Oh, Gracie," she said to herself,
You're such an ugly mouse."

And a voice said from behind,
"Well, you're right and you're wrong.
If you pin those ears down,
They wouldn't be so long."

A little yellow bird
Came and sat on her shoulder.
And how to hide her ears
Is just what he told her.

At the very same time,
Grant was sitting under a tree.
"My feet are the worst,
I wish I was anyone but me."

"Well, I'm not that skilled,"
The same voice whispered to him.
"But I know what to do.
I'll help you blend right in."

That very next morning,
When the friends arrived at school,
There was something different,
And the teacher noticed too.

Gracie & Grant's Big Win

Gracie's ears had started hurting,
No, they didn't feel good.
They were pinned to her head,
But she wished that they stood.

Grant's pants covered his feet,
But that made him fall even more!
He liked that no one stared,
But he kept hitting the floor!

As the class ran out to play,
The teacher held back the two.
The friends kept their heads down,
They both felt real blue.

"Now, Gracie, Grant,"
The teacher said with a sigh,
"I've noticed you've changed,
And I'd like to know why."

Gracie & Grant's Big Win

"Grant called my ears ugly!"
"Gracie made fun of my feet!"
"And I thought if I changed,
Then maybe I'd be neat."

"Oh, Gracie and Grant,
Don't be silly, you're both great!
Everyone is different.
Some grow fast, some grow late."

The teacher went on,
"You two are the best of friends.
Don't let words get between you,
Stick by each other till the end."

The friends both sadly
Nodded their heads
They saw everyone on the swings,
But wandered to the big field instead.

The friends were just about to make up,
When the little yellow bird flew down.
"Hey there, ugly ducklings,
Why the big frowns?"

As the bird landed with a plop,
Their world transformed once more.
Beneath the colors and flowers,
Something big was in store.

The friends saw right away
That their suits were on,
But this time it felt
Like they didn't belong.

Gracie just felt silly
With her ears standing tall.
And Grant was real nervous
That when he stepped he would fall.

Gracie & Grant's Big Win

The bird looked bigger as it said,
"Well don't you two just look sad.
I thought I told you to hide your flaws,
Then it wouldn't be so bad."

And as the friends felt worse,
The bird continued to grow.
It fed off their doubt,
And the friends didn't even know.

The feathers were gone.
In their place were thick scales.
The beak had even sharpened.
It had talons and razor tails!

"You're right where I want you,"
The monster said, at its worst.
"So prepare for your doom.
None of your powers will work!"

Gracie & Grant's Big Win

The friends trembled in fear,
They didn't know how to fight!
They both ran and hid,
They just didn't feel right.

They went into the forest
And hid under a tree.
"I'll try my No Voice," Gracie said,
"It'll work, you'll see!"

She leaped out towards the beast,
And she shouted her "NO!"
It staggered the beast,
But it swung at her with a blow!

Grant jumped out too,
And stopped its tail with his shield,
But it knocked them both back
And they flew across the whole field!

"Gracie," Grant said,
As he brushed off the blow,
"I think your ears are cool,
And I just like when they show."

"Really?" Gracie asked.
Then she smiled bright!
"I wish I had big feet,
You can kick a ball out of sight!"

The friends started laughing,
They no longer felt down.
They were back in the game,
It was time for the second round!

The monster flew toward them,
But the friends moved fast.
They worked together
And prepared a great blast!

"You're ugly and dumb!"
The monster shrieked as it flew.
But Gracie said "No" to her doubt
And Grant blocked the words too!

With Gracie's great big, "NO!"
And Grant's beam right beside,
They blasted the monster
And it went soaring into the sky!

Gracie & Grant's Big Win

The friends laughed with joy,
Their friendship stronger than ever.
They flew through their land
And valued self-confidence forever.

Has anyone ever said something
to make you feel bad?
Is there something about yourself
that you wish was different?
Draw a picture or write it down,
and know that our differences
make us unique and special!

Say: So, in the story, Gracie and Grant both felt like they were different in some ways. In what way did Grant feel different? In what way did Gracie feel different?

Teacher's note: Students will give examples and teacher will write responses on the board.

 Say: Both Gracie and Grant are very *unique*. Does anyone know what the word "unique" means?

 Say: To be unique means that you are not typical, or a bit unusual. It means that there is no one else like you because you are special. I want you to think about how you are unique and tell a friend quietly what makes you different.

Part 2: Puzzle Activity (10 minutes)

 Say: I want you to think about the things that make you unique. I want to show you this puzzle. (Teacher holds up the teacher example of a puzzle piece.) This is a puzzle piece that represents who I am and how I am unique. Each piece of a real puzzle is unique or different, yet when you put them all together they make an amazing picture. Today, you are going to make your own puzzle piece that shows how unique you are. When you are finished we will put all the pieces together to make a big puzzle.

Teacher's note: Give each student a pre-cut puzzle piece. Students can use markers, crayons, or anything else to color their puzzle piece or to make drawings to represent their uniqueness. At the end, teacher will encourage a few students to share their puzzle piece with the class so that they can show each other what they like about themselves.

 Say: Everyone is different and unique in their own way. The most important thing is to be confident in who you are, because you are special.

Gracie & Grant's Big Win

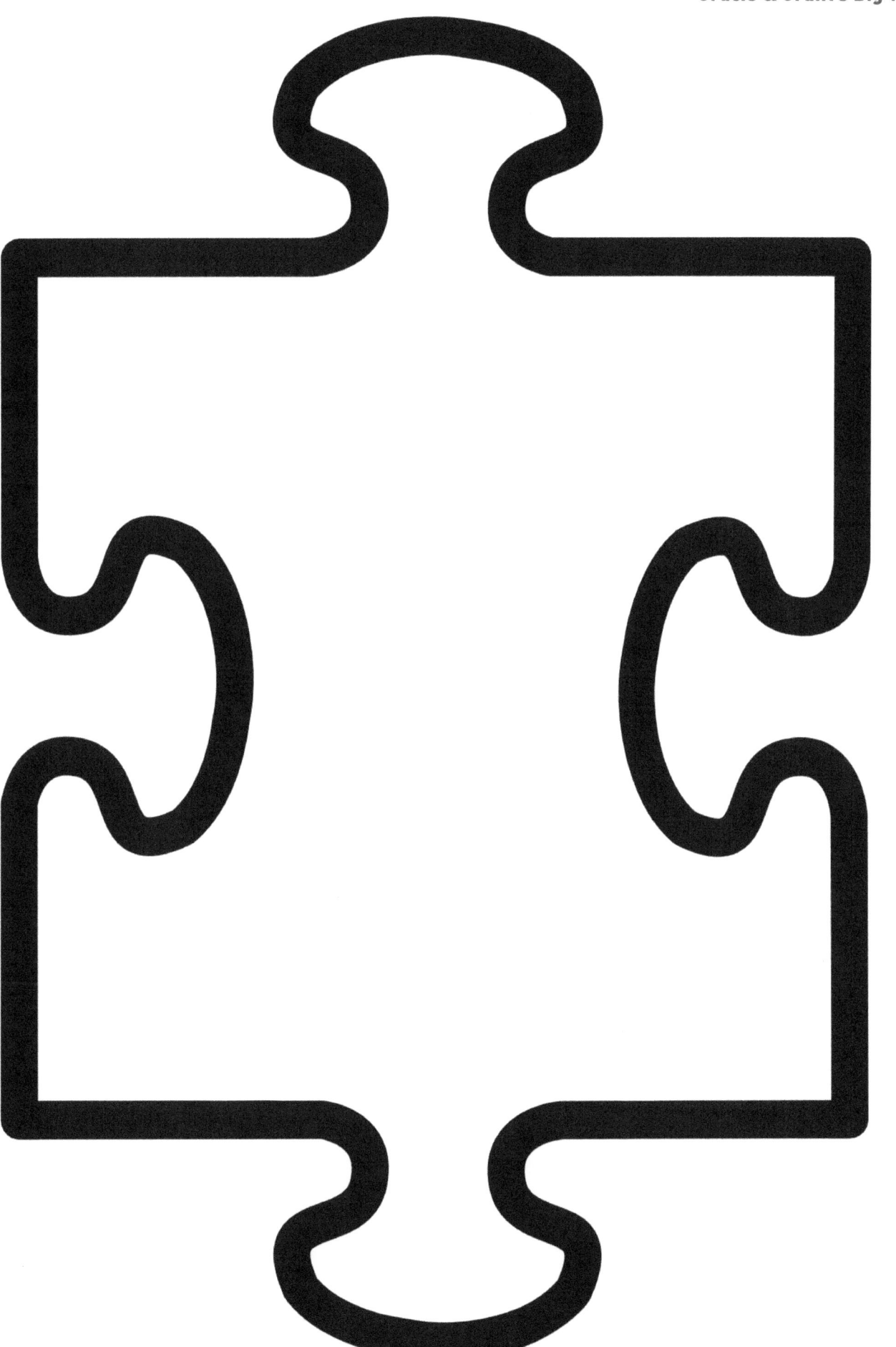

71

Lesson # 2: Wall of Compliments

Teacher's Overview

Lesson time: 33 minutesPreparation time: 15 minutes

Lesson Summary
In this lesson, students will learn to look for the good in other people. They will learn that a compliment can make a person feel important and special (improve self-confidence).

Lesson Objectives

By the end of this lesson, students will be able to:
1. Understand that a compliment is saying something nice about someone else.
2. Understand that compliments make other people feel special.

Materials Provided	Materials Needed
Gracie & Grant's Big Win book	Sentence starters (if needed) for the "Wall of Compliments" Markers/Crayons Colored paper

Teacher Preparation	Room Setup
Prepare at least one compliment for each of your students to share with the class at the beginning of the lesson. Cut colored paper in half or fourths. This will be used for the "Wall of Compliments." If needed, provide sentence starters such as, "_____ is good at _____" or, "I enjoy _____ because _____."	Desks or tables for writing activity

Part 1: What Does a Compliment Sound Like? (15 minutes)

Teacher begins by going around the room verbally giving each student a compliment.

 Say: Raise your hand and tell me how you felt after I told you something good about yourself?

Teacher's note: Allow several students to respond to the question.

Listen for: Happy, special, important, etc. . . .

 Say: When I was going around the room and telling you something good about yourself, I was giving each of you a compliment. Have you heard that word before?

Teacher's note: Allow several students to respond to the question.

Say: A compliment is a way to show kindness to others. It makes you and the person receiving the compliment feel good inside.

Say: The book we read yesterday, *Gracie & Grant's Big Win*, has two compliments in the story. Do you remember where they were found? Lets review where we found the compliments.

The compliments are found near the end of the story when Gracie and Grant are fighting off the bird.

> "Gracie," Grant said,
> As he brushed off the blow,
> "I think your ears are cool,
> And I just like when they show."
>
> "Really?" Gracie asked.
> Then she smiled bright!
> "I wish I had big feet,
> You can kick a ball out of sight!"
>
> The friends started laughing,
> They no longer felt down.
> They were back in the game,
> It was time for the second round!

Say: Based on what we just read, how did the compliments make Gracie and Grant feel? What were they able to do after they felt better about themselves?

Listen for: They felt better about themselves. They were stronger, braver, etc. . . . They had the confidence to fight off the bird.

Gracie & Grant's Big Win

Part 2: Drawing (15 minutes)

Teacher's note: Give each student a colored piece of paper. Students will come up with a compliment for another student in the classroom. Teacher may want to partner students so that each student gives and receives a compliment. Give sentence starters to those students that need them.

Say: We will get the chance to give and recieve compliments today. You will write a compliment on your paper. We will make a "Wall of Compliments" for our classroom to remember the good things we see in each other. When you and your partner are finished, share your compliment with your partner.

Teacher's note: Give students time to finish their writing. Once students share their compliment with their partner, have a few students volunteer to read their compliment out loud to the class.

Review/Check for Knowledge (3 minutes)

Say: Thank you for working so diligently on your compliments today. How did you feel when your partner complimented you? How did you feel when you complimented your partner?

It is important to notice the people around us and to let them know we appreciate them. Everyone is different but we all bring something good and exciting to the classroom.

FIND YOUR VOICE

Supplemental Resources

Supplemental Resource

Gracie & Grant's Big Win Coloring Book

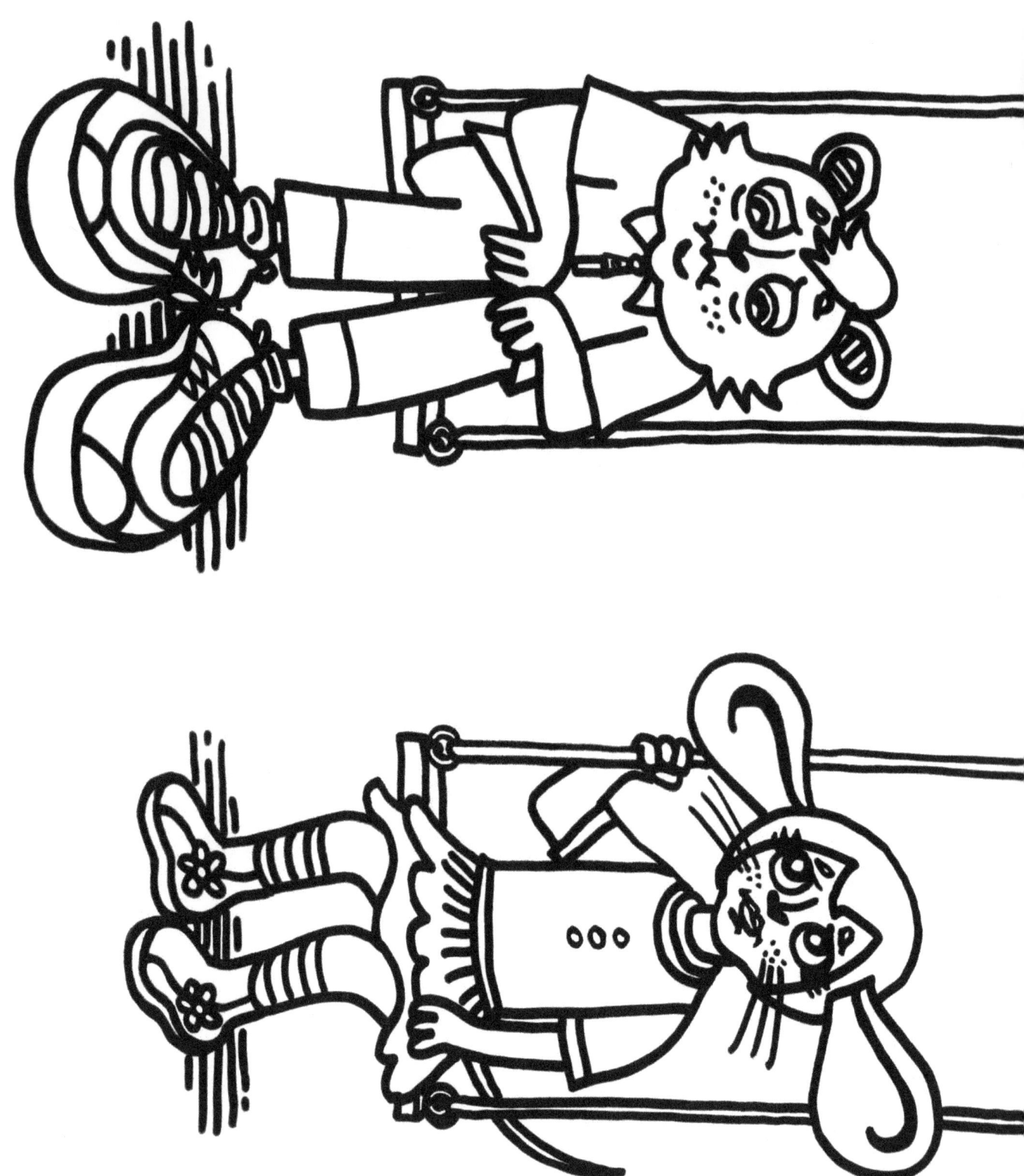

Books by Angela Williams

Loving Me: After Abuse
From Sorrows to Sapphires, Angela Williams's Memoir

Interactive Workbooks—Adults

Healing
Pathway to Healing, Guide to Healing
True Intimacy
Shattering the Shame
Unveiling Child Sexual Abuse

Prevention
Tough Talk to Tender Hearts
The Grooming Mystery
Single Parenting Solutions
Courage to Speak

Children's Books (Ages 5–10)
Gracie Finds Her Voice
Grant Gets His Shield
Gracie and Grant's Big Win
Gracie and Grant's Big Win Coloring Book
Find Your Voice Curriculum Book

Angela's Voice

Angela's Voice is dedicated to developing, distributing, and endorsing valuable resources in the awareness, prevention, and healing of child sexual abuse. The materials, though specific for survivors of child sexual abuse, also benefit any abuse survivor and help protect children by teaching them how to defend themselves from abusive behavior. Founder Angela Williams, MFP, is a survivor-turned-advocate who shares a powerful message of triumph over tragedy by sharing her vulnerable and candid voice about her abuse trauma, her pain, her struggles, and her journey to healing in hopes that it may help other survivors expedite their healing journey.

Williams has devoted years to providing awareness, prevention, and healing programs through her advocacy work. Williams has captivated audiences with her powerful message of triumph over tragedy as a victim of childhood physical and sexual abuse. At age seventeen, she attempted suicide, and that day was the end of her torment and the beginning of a journey to healing. She is a crusader for change and dedicates her life to eradicate child sexual abuse. She holds a master's in forensic psychology with a concentration in child abuse. Williams is a powerful messenger, appearing in national and international news and documentaries. She has been successful in state legislative reform and national policy work and served on the Policy Committee of the National Coalition to Prevent Child Sexual Abuse and Exploitation. She has received numerous accolades and awards for her work, including her collection of books that have valuable lessons for survivors of all ages.

www.ingramcontent.com/pod-product-compliance
Lightning Source LLC
Chambersburg PA
CBHW040002080526
44586CB00027B/2855